Table of Contents

THIS BOOK IS DEDICATED TO THE Stephen G. family, (Author) Stephen G.

THIS BOOK IS DEDICATED TO THE Stephen G. family, (Author) Stephen G.

Spirits of the Southwest: Ghost Tours and Paranormal Adventures in Albuquerque

Chapter 1: Introduction to Albuquerque's Haunted Heritage

The Rich History of Albuquerque

Albuquerque, New Mexico, is a city steeped in a rich tapestry of history that intertwines Native American, Spanish, and Mexican influences. Established in 1706, the city was named after the Duke of Alburquerque, a Spanish nobleman. Its strategic location along the Rio Grande made it an essential hub for trade and cultural exchange, attracting settlers, traders, and explorers from various backgrounds. The area was originally inhabited by the Pueblo Indians, whose traditions and spiritual beliefs continue to influence the region today. The melding of these diverse cultures has forged a unique identity for Albuquerque that is deeply embedded in its historical narrative.

Throughout the 18th and 19th centuries, Albuquerque grew as a center for agriculture and commerce. The introduction of the railroad in the late 1800s further accelerated its development, transforming it into a vital junction for travelers and goods. The architectural landscape of Albuquerque reflects this evolution, showcasing a blend of adobe structures, Victorian homes, and modern developments. Each building tells a story, with many sites now considered haunted due to their long-standing history. Ghost tours in Albuquerque often highlight these locations, where the past continues to echo through the present, inviting visitors to explore the stories of the souls who once inhabited these spaces.

Albuquerque's rich history is also marked by significant events that have shaped its cultural landscape. The city played a pivotal role during the Mexican-American War and the subsequent Treaty of Guadalupe Hidalgo, which altered territorial boundaries and transformed the lives of its residents. This historical backdrop contributes to the ghostly tales that abound in the area. Locations such as the Old Town Plaza and the Albuquerque Museum are not only historical sites but also hotspots for paranormal activity, attracting enthusiasts eager to connect with the spirits of the past.

The influence of Native American spirituality is palpable in Albuquerque, with the nearby pueblos maintaining their customs and ceremonies. These ancient traditions add another layer to the city's ghostly lore, as many believe that the spirits of ancestors linger in the lands they once inhabited. Ghost tours often delve into these spiritual beliefs, offering insights into the rituals and stories that have been passed down through generations. Visitors are encouraged to engage with this aspect of history, deepening their understanding of the cultural significance of the area.

As modern Albuquerque continues to thrive as a vibrant city, its historical roots remain a crucial part of its charm. The intersections of past and present create a unique atmosphere, particularly for those interested in paranormal experiences. Whether exploring the haunted halls of historic hotels or wandering through the eerie streets of Old Town, adventurers can expect to encounter the spirits that linger in the shadows. The rich history of Albuquerque serves as a backdrop for these encounters, inviting all who visit to connect with the ghosts of its storied past.

Folklore and Legends of the Southwest

The Southwest is a rich tapestry of folklore and legends, deeply woven into the cultural fabric of the region. The stories told here often revolve around the mystical and the supernatural, reflecting the diverse heritage of Native American tribes, Spanish settlers, and later European immigrants. These tales are not merely entertaining; they serve as cautionary tales, lessons in morality, and explanations for the unexplainable. In Albuquerque, these legends come alive, offering visitors a glimpse into the mystical side of the city that lies just beneath its vibrant surface.

One of the most prevalent figures in Southwest folklore is La Llorona, or the Weeping Woman. This tragic spirit reportedly wanders the riverside, mourning her lost children. According to legend, La Llorona was a beautiful woman who drowned her children in a fit of rage and now spends eternity searching for them, luring unsuspecting victims to their doom. Variations of her story can be found throughout Latin America, but in Albuquerque, her presence is felt particularly strong along the Rio Grande, where locals claim to hear her cries echoing in the night. This haunting tale serves as a reminder of the consequences of unchecked emotion, making it a staple of ghost tours in the area.

Another captivating legend is that of the Sandia Mountains, which are believed to be home to numerous spirits and supernatural occurrences. Many Native American tribes regard these mountains as sacred, and stories abound of ancestral spirits watching over the land. Hikers and outdoor enthusiasts often report eerie feelings while traversing the trails, claiming to see ghostly figures or hear whispers in the wind. These experiences add an ethereal layer to the beauty of the landscape, inviting visitors to respect the history and stories that have been passed down through generations.

The story of the "Headless Horseman of the Old Town" is another notorious tale that draws the attention of both locals and tourists alike. According to this legend, a soldier who was wronged in love met a gruesome fate and now roams Old Town Albuquerque without his head. Visitors claim to have seen his ghostly figure galloping through the streets, primarily on moonlit nights. This narrative not only captivates the imagination but also highlights the historical tensions and romantic entanglements of the past, enriching the experience of exploring the old adobe buildings and plazas of the city.

As one delves deeper into the folklore of the Southwest, it becomes clear that these stories are more than just ghostly tales; they are reflections of the region's history, struggles, and beliefs. Each legend offers a unique perspective on the cultures that have shaped Albuquerque, making it a prime location for those interested in paranormal experiences. Visitors to the city can engage with these stories through ghost tours, which not only provide thrilling encounters but also educate participants about the rich heritage that continues to influence the area today. Through these narratives, the spirits of the Southwest remain alive, inviting all who venture here to listen closely to the echoes of the past.

Understanding Paranormal Activity

Paranormal activity refers to events and phenomena that cannot be explained by known scientific laws or principles. This includes experiences such as ghost sightings, unexplained noises, and feelings of being watched or touched. Understanding paranormal activity requires an exploration of various perspectives, including historical accounts, cultural beliefs, and personal experiences. In Albuquerque, a city rich in history and folklore, the study of paranormal activity is particularly intriguing, intertwining the tales of its past with the experiences of those who walk its haunted streets.

Many residents and visitors report experiences that defy logical explanation. These experiences often occur in locations steeped in history, where the energy of past events seems to linger. In Albuquerque, sites like the Old Town Plaza and the Sandia Mountains are frequently mentioned in ghost stories. The narratives surrounding these locations not only provide entertainment but also reflect the complexities of human emotions and the unresolved issues that may perpetuate these paranormal encounters. By examining the history of these sites, one can gain insight into the reasons behind the reported phenomena.

Cultural beliefs play a significant role in shaping perceptions of paranormal activity. In the Southwest, Native American traditions often encompass a deep connection to the spiritual world, viewing the presence of spirits as a natural aspect of existence. This perspective can enhance the understanding of ghostly encounters, as many visitors find their experiences influenced by the rich tapestry of local culture. The blending of different traditions in Albuquerque creates a unique environment where various interpretations of the paranormal coexist, leading to a diverse range of experiences and beliefs.

The personal experiences of individuals also contribute significantly to the understanding of paranormal activity. Many who partake in ghost tours in Albuquerque share their stories of eerie encounters, often recounting feelings of sudden coldness, the sensation of being watched, or even direct interactions with spirits. These narratives can evoke a sense of connection to the past, allowing individuals to explore their own beliefs about life after death and the nature of existence. As participants engage with the tour guides and fellow attendees, they often find common ground in their curiosity and fascination with the unexplained.

In conclusion, understanding paranormal activity in Albuquerque involves an interplay of history, culture, and personal experience. The city serves as a living tapestry of ghostly tales and supernatural phenomena, inviting both skeptics and believers to explore its haunted locations. As visitors embark on ghost tours and paranormal adventures, they not only seek thrills but also a deeper understanding of the mysterious forces that may inhabit the world around them. This exploration can lead to a greater appreciation for the stories that shape our understanding of the past and the unseen elements that may continue to influence our lives.

Chapter 2: The Ghost Tours of Albuquerque

Overview of Ghost Tours

Ghost tours have become a popular attraction in cities with rich histories and vibrant folklore, and Albuquerque is no exception. These tours offer a unique opportunity for participants to delve into the city's past while exploring its haunted locations. The blend of history, mystery, and the supernatural captivates both locals and visitors alike, making ghost tours an essential part of the Albuquerque experience. Whether you are a skeptic or a believer, these adventures promise an engaging exploration of the paranormal.

In Albuquerque, ghost tours typically lead participants through historic neighborhoods, stopping at significant sites that are believed to harbor spirits. The Old Town area, with its adobe buildings and centuries-old history, is a focal point for many tours. Visitors hear chilling tales of hauntings and ghostly encounters, often paired with historical anecdotes that provide context to the spectral stories. This intertwining of history and the supernatural creates a fascinating narrative that enhances the overall experience.

Many ghost tours in Albuquerque also incorporate local legends and folklore into their storytelling. The tales often feature prominent figures from the city's past, such as soldiers, settlers, and even Native American spirits. These narratives not only entertain but also educate participants about the cultural and historical tapestry of the region. The guides, often passionate about the paranormal, weave these stories with a sense of theatricality, making each tour a memorable and immersive experience.

The appeal of ghost tours extends beyond mere thrills; they serve as a platform for social interaction. Participants often engage with one another, sharing their own experiences and thoughts on the paranormal. This communal aspect enhances the adventure, as guests bond over shared fascination and curiosity. Many tours also provide opportunities for photography, allowing participants to capture the ambiance of the haunted locations and perhaps even document any unexpected phenomena.

In conclusion, ghost tours in Albuquerque offer a unique blend of history, storytelling, and community engagement, making them a must-try for both residents and visitors. These tours not only illuminate the darker aspects of the city's history but also invite participants to engage with the supernatural in a way that is both entertaining and informative. For anyone seeking a memorable experience that combines adventure with a touch of the eerie, Albuquerque's ghost tours present an enticing option.

Popular Ghost Tour Companies

When exploring the haunted history of Albuquerque, several ghost tour companies stand out for their engaging narratives and immersive experiences. These companies offer a unique blend of local folklore, historical context, and paranormal investigation, making them popular choices for both tourists and locals alike. Each company has its own distinctive approach, catering to various interests and levels of enthusiasm for the supernatural.

One of the most well-known ghost tour companies in Albuquerque is Albuquerque Ghost Tours. This company provides guided evening tours that delve into the city's rich history and its many haunted locations. Participants can expect to hear chilling tales of ghostly encounters while visiting sites like the Old Town Plaza and the San Felipe de Neri Church. The knowledgeable guides not only share haunting stories but also offer insights into the historical significance of each location, creating a well-rounded experience.

Another popular option is the Ghosts of Albuquerque tour, which focuses on the darker side of the city's past. This tour takes participants through the historic district, exploring locations tied to tragic events and untimely deaths. The guides, often equipped with ghost-hunting tools, engage guests with interactive storytelling that encourages them to share their own ghostly experiences. This hands-on approach adds an exciting layer of participation for those eager to connect with the paranormal.

For those seeking a more theatrical experience, the Haunted History Tours offer a unique twist. These tours combine historical narratives with elements of performance, often featuring actors who portray characters from Albuquerque's past. This blend of history and drama captivates participants, making for an entertaining evening filled with suspense and intrigue. The guides are adept at creating a spooky atmosphere, drawing visitors into the tales of hauntings and local legends.

Lastly, for a more in-depth exploration of the paranormal, the Paranormal Adventures company provides ghost hunting experiences. Participants can join investigations at some of Albuquerque's most haunted sites, using ghost-hunting equipment to seek evidence of the supernatural. This hands-on approach appeals to those who wish to delve deeper into the paranormal realm, providing an unforgettable experience that combines thrill and curiosity. Each of these companies contributes to the vibrant tapestry of ghost tourism in Albuquerque, ensuring that visitors leave with unforgettable memories of the city's spectral past.

What to Expect on a Ghost Tour

When embarking on a ghost tour in Albuquerque, participants can expect an immersive experience that blends history, folklore, and the supernatural. Each tour typically begins with a gathering point where guests meet their guide, often an experienced storyteller with a passion for the paranormal. As the group assembles, there is an air of anticipation, with participants sharing their own ghostly encounters or expressing curiosity about what lies ahead. The guide usually sets the tone by explaining the structure of the tour, addressing safety protocols, and providing a brief overview of the haunted locations on the itinerary.

The heart of a ghost tour is the exploration of historically significant sites, many of which are steeped in local legends and eerie tales. In Albuquerque, locations such as the Old Town Plaza or the San Felipe de Neri Church serve as backdrops for chilling stories of spirits, tragic events, and unexplained phenomena. As the group navigates through these areas, the guide recounts gripping narratives that might include accounts of past residents, unsolved mysteries, or the cultural significance of the sites. This storytelling aspect not only engages the participants but also enriches their understanding of Albuquerque's rich history and the events that have shaped its haunted reputation.

Participants should also be prepared for varying levels of interaction during the tour. Some guides encourage guests to share their own ghost stories or ask questions, creating a more dynamic experience. Others may incorporate ghost-hunting tools, such as EMF detectors or spirit boxes, allowing guests to engage in a hands-on investigation of the paranormal. This interactive element can heighten the excitement and intrigue, making it a memorable experience for those seeking to connect with the supernatural.

The atmosphere during a ghost tour is often enhanced by the time of day. Many tours occur in the evening, when the fading light casts shadows and the cool night air adds to the eerie ambiance. Participants may find themselves walking along dimly lit streets or peering into historic buildings, all while listening to ghostly tales that seem to come alive in the dark. The setting creates a sense of mystery and suspense, heightening the thrill of possibly encountering something otherworldly.

Finally, guests can expect a sense of camaraderie and shared experience among fellow participants. Ghost tours attract a diverse crowd, including locals and tourists alike, all united by a common interest in the paranormal. As the night unfolds, stories and laughter often flow, fostering connections between strangers. This communal aspect adds to the enjoyment of the tour, making it more than just a simple exploration of haunted sites; it becomes a memorable adventure filled with shared thrills, chills, and perhaps a newfound fascination with the spirits that linger in Albuquerque.

Chapter 3: Historic Locations and Their Hauntings

Old Town Albuquerque

Old Town Albuquerque, a historic district that dates back to the early 18th century, serves as a captivating entry point into the rich tapestry of New Mexico's culture and history. The original Spanish colonial settlement, with its adobe buildings and vibrant plazas, invites visitors to explore a world where the past and present intertwine seamlessly. The area is not only a hub for unique shopping and dining but also a focal point for ghost tours and paranormal investigations, offering a glimpse into the spectral tales that haunt its storied streets.

The architecture of Old Town reflects its diverse cultural influences, from Native American to Spanish colonial. As the sun sets, the ambience shifts, and the soft glow of lanterns casts long shadows, creating an eerie yet enchanting atmosphere.

Visitors often report strange occurrences, such as inexplicable cold spots and the sensation of being watched, as they wander through the narrow streets. Many ghost tours guide participants through these historic pathways, sharing spine-chilling stories of apparitions and hauntings that have been passed down through generations.

One of the most famous haunted locations in Old Town is the San Felipe de Neri Church, which has stood since 1793. The church is not only a place of worship but also a site of numerous ghostly encounters. Tour guides recount tales of a former priest who is said to still roam the premises, offering blessings to those he encounters. The church's historic significance and the lingering energy from centuries of congregation contribute to its reputation as a hotspot for paranormal activity, drawing both skeptics and believers alike.

Another notable location is the Old Town Plaza, where visitors often experience a sense of nostalgia and unease. Many claim to hear whispers in the night or catch glimpses of shadowy figures darting between the trees. Local lore suggests that the spirits of those who lived and loved in Old Town continue to linger, their stories woven into the very fabric of the plaza. Ghost tours frequently pause here to share chilling accounts of the area's past, enriching the experience with historical context and personal anecdotes from those who have encountered the supernatural.

As visitors stroll through Old Town Albuquerque, they are not merely exploring a historic site; they are stepping into a living narrative filled with mystery and intrigue. The combination of rich history, architectural beauty, and ghostly tales creates an immersive experience that captivates the imagination. Whether one is a seasoned ghost hunter or a curious traveler, Old Town offers an unforgettable journey into the heart of New Mexico's haunted heritage, making it a must-visit destination for those seeking both adventure and a connection to the otherworldly.

The KiMo Theatre

The KiMo Theatre, a storied landmark in Albuquerque, holds a significant place in the city's cultural and historical landscape. Built in the early 1920s, it was designed in the Pueblo Deco style, a unique architectural blend that reflects the region's Native American heritage and the Art Deco movement. The theatre quickly became a hub for entertainment, showcasing everything from films to live performances. Its vibrant interior, adorned with intricate murals and a stunning chandelier, has captivated audiences for generations, making it not only a venue for the arts but also a cherished community gathering spot.

As with many historic venues, the KiMo Theatre has its share of ghostly tales that intrigue both locals and visitors alike. Numerous reports of paranormal activity have been documented over the years, with theater staff and patrons recounting experiences that range from disembodied voices to the sensation of being watched. Some claim to have seen shadowy figures moving through the aisles or felt sudden drops in temperature, particularly in the upper levels of the theatre. These accounts have contributed to the KiMo's reputation as one of Albuquerque's most haunted locations.

One of the most notable spirits associated with the KiMo is said to be that of a young girl named "Sophie." Legend has it that she tragically lost her life in a fire that occurred during a performance in the early years of the theatre's operation. Since then, visitors have reported hearing her laughter echoing through the halls and occasionally catching glimpses of a small figure darting between the seats. This playful spirit has become a part of the theatre's lore, drawing ghost hunters and curious tourists eager to experience the supernatural for themselves.

The KiMo Theatre is not only a hotspot for ghostly encounters but also serves as a focal point for paranormal investigations. Many ghost tours in Albuquerque include this iconic venue on their itineraries, offering participants a chance to explore its haunted corners. Enthusiasts equipped with ghost-hunting tools often gather in the theatre to seek evidence of the afterlife. Guided tours provide insight into the theatre's history, while also sharing chilling stories that heighten the thrill of the experience. This combination of history and haunting makes the KiMo a must-visit for those intrigued by the paranormal.

Visiting the KiMo Theatre offers more than just the chance to encounter spirits; it provides an opportunity to appreciate a piece of Albuquerque's rich heritage. The venue hosts a variety of events, including film screenings, live performances, and community gatherings, allowing guests to immerse themselves in both the cultural and mystical aspects of the theatre. For those interested in the paranormal, the KiMo Theatre stands as a testament to the enduring connection between the living and the spirits that linger in this vibrant space, making it an essential stop on any ghost tour in the Southwest.

The Albuquerque Museum

The Albuquerque Museum, located in the heart of the city, serves as a cultural hub that showcases the rich history and artistic heritage of the region. Established in 1967, it is dedicated to preserving and interpreting the diverse narratives that have shaped Albuquerque and the surrounding areas. Visitors are greeted by a striking blend of contemporary and traditional architecture, creating an inviting atmosphere for exploration. The museum's extensive collection includes over 7,000 works of art, as well as historical artifacts that provide insight into the Native American, Hispanic, and Anglo influences on the area's development.

In addition to its impressive art and historical collections, the Albuquerque Museum is known for hosting a variety of temporary exhibits that delve into specific themes or contemporary issues. These rotating exhibits often include local artists and community projects, fostering a sense of connection between the museum and the residents of Albuquerque. Each exhibit invites visitors to engage with the stories and experiences that have shaped the city's identity, making it an essential stop for anyone interested in the cultural landscape of the Southwest.

For those intrigued by the paranormal, the Albuquerque Museum holds its own set of ghostly tales. As a site steeped in history, it is not surprising that visitors and staff alike have reported unexplained occurrences. Some claim to have felt sudden drops in temperature in certain galleries, while others have experienced fleeting shadows or heard whispers in the quiet halls. These unsettling experiences complement the museum's narrative of the past, suggesting that the spirits of those who have walked its paths may still linger among the artworks and artifacts.

The museum also offers special events and programs that cater to those interested in the supernatural. Ghost tours and themed nights provide an engaging way to explore the building's history and the legends associated with it. Participants can listen to accounts of paranormal encounters while walking through the galleries, creating an immersive experience that blends art appreciation with the thrill of ghost hunting. These events are particularly popular around Halloween, drawing in both locals and tourists eager to explore the mysterious side of the museum.

In conclusion, the Albuquerque Museum stands as a vibrant testament to the city's artistic and historical legacy, while also serving as a canvas for paranormal exploration. For adults and vacationers seeking a unique blend of culture and the supernatural, the museum offers a captivating experience. Whether one is admiring the artworks, learning about the region's past, or delving into ghostly legends, the Albuquerque Museum provides a distinctive glimpse into the spirits of the Southwest.

The Hotel Andaluz

The Hotel Andaluz, a historic gem nestled in the heart of Albuquerque, offers visitors a unique blend of rich history and paranormal intrigue. Originally built in 1925 as the Alvarado Hotel, it was designed by famed architect Mary Colter. The hotel served as a bustling hub for travelers and locals alike, thanks to its prime location near the Santa Fe Railroad. Over the decades, the building underwent significant transformations, but its architectural beauty and historic significance remain intact, making it a must-visit destination for those interested in both history and the supernatural.

Guests of the Hotel Andaluz often recount experiences that cannot be easily explained. Many have reported hearing unexplained noises, such as footsteps echoing down the hallways or the sound of children laughing in empty rooms. These experiences are often attributed to the hotel's storied past, where it has seen countless guests pass through its doors. The spirit of a former bellboy is said to roam the lobby, and several visitors claim to have encountered him while checking in. His presence, while unsettling to some, adds to the hotel's charm and allure for those seeking a ghostly encounter.

The hotel's enchanting ambiance is further enhanced by its beautiful Spanish-Moorish architecture and intricate décor. The lobby, adorned with stunning chandeliers and rich textiles, sets the stage for an enchanting atmosphere. Many guests find themselves drawn to the rooftop terrace, which offers breathtaking views of Albuquerque and the Sandia Mountains. As night falls, the terrace transforms into a serene setting, where guests often share ghost stories and experiences, forging connections over the eerie tales that surround the hotel.

For those interested in a more structured exploration of the paranormal, the Hotel Andaluz offers guided ghost tours. These tours delve into the hotel's history, revealing secrets and stories that have shaped its legacy. Participants are led through the hotel's most haunted areas, allowing them to experience the unexplained phenomena firsthand. The knowledgeable guides share chilling accounts of encounters and sightings, creating an immersive experience for those curious about the supernatural.

Staying at the Hotel Andaluz not only provides a comfortable and luxurious retreat but also an opportunity to engage with the spectral side of Albuquerque. Whether you are a seasoned ghost hunter or simply curious about the beyond, the hotel serves as a perfect base for exploring the paranormal. Its enchanting history, combined with the reported ghostly encounters, makes it a noteworthy destination for anyone seeking adventure in the Southwest.

Chapter 4: Paranormal Experiences and Investigations

Introduction to Paranormal Investigations

Paranormal investigations have intrigued and captivated individuals for centuries, blending the realms of mystery, history, and the supernatural. In Albuquerque, a city rich with cultural heritage and a tapestry of ghostly tales, paranormal investigations offer a unique way to explore the unknown. As you embark on this journey, you will engage with the stories of those who have come before us, delving into the experiences that continue to resonate in the spirits that inhabit the area.

The allure of paranormal investigations stems from a deep-seated curiosity about life after death and the possibility of communicating with entities from beyond our physical realm. In Albuquerque, this curiosity is heightened by the city's diverse history, encompassing Native American traditions, Spanish colonization, and more recent developments. Each layer of history contributes to the rich tapestry of ghostly lore, making the city a fascinating backdrop for those interested in uncovering the mysteries that lie beneath the surface.

As you participate in paranormal investigations, you will utilize a variety of tools and techniques designed to detect supernatural activity. From EVP (Electronic Voice Phenomena) recorders to infrared cameras, these instruments help investigators capture evidence of ghostly presences. Many tours incorporate these tools, allowing participants to engage actively in the process. This interactive experience transforms what could be a passive observation into a thrilling adventure, where every shadow and sound may lead to a deeper understanding of the paranormal.

In addition to the equipment used, the stories that accompany each investigation are equally compelling. Each haunted location in Albuquerque has its own unique narrative, often tied to historical events or significant figures. From the haunted halls of the Albuquerque Old Town to the eerie whispers in the shadows of local cemeteries, these tales enrich the experience and provide context for the phenomena encountered. Participants not only seek to observe the unexplained but also to connect with the history and emotions associated with each site.

Ultimately, paranormal investigations in Albuquerque serve as both an adventure and an opportunity for personal reflection. Whether you are a seasoned ghost hunter or a newcomer to the world of the supernatural, exploring these haunted locations invites you to question your beliefs about life, death, and everything in between. As you navigate the city's ghostly past, you may find yourself touched by the stories of the spirits that linger, creating lasting memories and perhaps a newfound appreciation for the mysteries that surround us.

Tools of the Trade

When embarking on ghost tours and paranormal adventures in Albuquerque, having the right tools can significantly enhance the experience. These tools range from traditional items used by ghost hunters to more modern technological gadgets that help in uncovering the unseen. Familiarity with these instruments not only aids in the exploration of haunted locations but also deepens the understanding of local folklore and history, making the tour more engaging for participants.

One of the most iconic tools in the paranormal investigator's arsenal is the EMF meter. This device detects electromagnetic fields and is often associated with the presence of spirits. Paranormal enthusiasts believe that fluctuations in electromagnetic fields can indicate ghostly activity. On ghost tours, guides may demonstrate how to use an EMF meter, allowing participants to engage with the experience actively. This hands-on approach can heighten the sense of adventure and curiosity, as guests may find themselves intrigued by the readings they observe in reputedly haunted sites.

Another essential tool is the spirit box, a device that scans radio frequencies to capture snippets of audio that may contain messages from the spirit world. During tours, guides may utilize spirit boxes to facilitate communication with potential paranormal entities. Participants often find this method thrilling, as it provides a direct channel to the unknown. Listening for responses and deciphering the sounds can make for an exhilarating experience, fostering a deeper connection to the haunted locations in Albuquerque.

For those interested in capturing evidence of the paranormal, digital cameras and voice recorders are vital tools. Many ghost tours encourage guests to bring their own devices to document their experiences. Photographs taken in dimly lit areas may reveal orbs or unexplained anomalies that could suggest ghostly presences. Similarly, audio recorders can capture Electronic Voice Phenomena (EVPs), which are sounds that appear to be voices or messages from spirits. Sharing these findings among tour participants can lead to fascinating discussions and theories about the supernatural, enriching the overall experience.

Finally, incorporating traditional items like pendulums or tarot cards can add an intriguing dimension to the ghost tour experience. These tools are often used in spiritual practices and can serve as a means of divination or connection to the spirit realm. Some tours may offer participants the opportunity to use these tools, enhancing their journey into the mystical and unknown. Such practices invite a broader understanding of the cultural and spiritual significance of the Southwest, making the ghost tours not just an exploration of the paranormal, but also an immersion into the rich tapestry of local traditions and beliefs.

Notable Paranormal Investigations in Albuquerque

Albuquerque, with its rich history and diverse cultural heritage, has long been a hotspot for paranormal investigations. The city's blend of Native American, Spanish, and Anglo influences creates a unique backdrop for ghost stories and supernatural occurrences. One of the most notable investigations took place at the Old Town Plaza, a historic area that dates back to the 18th century. Investigators have reported numerous instances of ghostly apparitions, particularly in the San Felipe de Neri Church, where visitors have felt sudden drops in temperature and seen shadowy figures. These experiences have led to a deeper exploration of the church's history and the spirits thought to linger there.

Another prominent site of paranormal interest is the Albuquerque Public Library's Main Branch. Built in the mid-20th century, the library has become the focus of various investigations due to claims of unusual sounds and sightings. Investigators have recorded unexplained noises, believed by some to be the echoes of past patrons. Ghost hunters have also reported seeing flickering lights and cold spots throughout the building, particularly in the attic, where the library's archives are stored. These phenomena have intrigued both amateur and professional ghost hunters, prompting several organized paranormal tours that delve into the library's ghostly lore.

The Sandia Mountains, which overlook Albuquerque, harbor their own share of mysteries. The area is known for its breathtaking views and outdoor activities, but it also has a reputation for unexplained occurrences, including mysterious lights and eerie sounds. Paranormal investigators have flocked to the Sandia foothills to explore these phenomena, often conducting night-time vigils. Local legends speak of spirits of the indigenous peoples who once inhabited the region, adding a layer of cultural significance to the investigations. The combination of natural beauty and supernatural tales makes the Sandia Mountains a compelling site for those interested in the paranormal.

The historic Hotel Andaluz is another focal point for paranormal exploration in Albuquerque. This elegant hotel, which dates back to 1939, has been the subject of numerous ghost stories. Guests and staff have reported sightings of a female figure believed to be a former owner, as well as unexplained noises and items moving on their own. The hotel has embraced its haunted reputation, even offering ghost tours for those curious about its storied past. Investigators have found the hotel to be a treasure trove of paranormal activity, attracting both seasoned ghost hunters and curious tourists.

Lastly, the New Mexico Museum of Natural History and Science has also garnered attention for its potential paranormal activity. Visitors have reported ghostly sightings in the museum's various exhibits, particularly in the dinosaur section. Some staff members have recounted stories of objects being misplaced or moved and feelings of being watched. Paranormal teams have conducted investigations, utilizing electromagnetic field meters and other tools to capture evidence of the unexplained. The museum's blend of science and the supernatural offers a unique perspective on the paranormal, making it an essential stop for anyone interested in ghostly encounters in Albuquerque.

Chapter 5: Stories from the Spirits

Encounters at the Old Town Plaza

The Old Town Plaza in Albuquerque is steeped in history and mystery, making it a popular destination for ghost tours and paranormal enthusiasts. This historic area, founded in 1706, is not only the cultural heart of the city but also a hotspot for supernatural encounters. Visitors often report feelings of being watched, sudden drops in temperature, and unexplained sounds, particularly in the evening when the shadows grow long and the cobblestone streets are bathed in moonlight.

One of the most frequently mentioned spirits in the plaza is that of a young woman dressed in traditional Spanish attire. Many claim to have seen her wandering near the San Felipe de Neri Church, which dates back to 1793. Witnesses describe her as having a serene expression, often stopping to gaze at the church's façade, as if searching for something lost in time. Some have even reported that she seems to vanish when approached, leaving behind only the faint scent of jasmine, a fragrance closely associated with the region.

Another notable entity is the ghost of a 19th-century soldier, who is said to patrol the plaza, particularly around the old adobe buildings. His presence is often felt by those who linger too long in the shadows, where he allegedly appears as a flickering figure in the corner of the eye. Tour guides share stories of visitors who have felt a sudden chill or heard the distant sound of clinking spurs, heightening the sense of unease as they walk through the area. This soldier's spirit appears to be a guardian of the plaza, watching over the historical site and its patrons.

The Old Town Plaza is also home to a variety of unique shops and galleries, many of which are said to be haunted by former owners or patrons. Shopkeepers have reported inexplicable noises, such as footsteps echoing in empty rooms, or objects moving without explanation. One notable shop, devoted to local art and crafts, has a reputation for its playful spirit who reportedly enjoys rearranging merchandise and causing a ruckus at night. Such tales add an even deeper layer to the experience of wandering through the plaza, as visitors become attuned to the possibility of encountering the unseen.

As dusk falls and the plaza begins to quiet, the atmosphere shifts, inviting those with an adventurous spirit to explore its haunted corners. Ghost tours often culminate in the plaza, where storytellers share chilling tales and legends that have shaped the area's ghostly reputation. Whether you are a skeptic or a believer, the Old Town Plaza offers an enchanting experience filled with history, culture, and the tantalizing possibility of encountering the otherworldly. Visitors leave with not only memories of a beautiful location but also with stories of their own encounters, contributing to the ongoing tapestry of paranormal experiences in Albuquerque.

Ghostly Tales from Local Residents

In the vibrant city of Albuquerque, ghostly tales have become an integral part of its cultural tapestry. Local residents often share their eerie experiences, adding a layer of intrigue to the city's rich history. These stories not only entertain but also offer insight into the spiritual beliefs and folklore that have shaped the region. From haunted hotels to historic neighborhoods, the tales of the supernatural echo through the streets, inviting both locals and visitors to explore the unknown.

One of the most famous ghost stories comes from the Hotel Andaluz, a beautifully restored hotel that dates back to the 1930s. Guests and staff alike have reported sightings of a mysterious woman in a flowing white gown wandering the hallways. Some believe she is the spirit of a former hotel guest who met an untimely end. Witnesses describe feelings of a cold breeze when she is near, and some have even claimed to hear her soft whispers in the night. This legend has become a favorite topic among ghost tour guides, who recount the tale with a mix of reverence and excitement.

In the Old Town area, locals recount stories of the spirit of a young girl named La Llorona, who is said to haunt the banks of the Rio Grande. This tragic figure is part of a broader Mexican folklore, known for her weeping cries echoing through the night. Residents often claim to hear her sorrowful laments, especially during the full moon. This haunting tale serves as a reminder of the deep cultural roots that influence the ghost stories of Albuquerque, connecting the past with the present in a hauntingly beautiful way.

Another chilling account comes from the Albuquerque Rail Yard, where workers have reported strange occurrences during late-night shifts. Shadows darting across the platforms and the sound of footsteps echoing in empty spaces have led to speculation about the spirits of railroad workers from bygone eras. Some employees have even claimed to see apparitions, dressed in old-fashioned attire, going about their daily routines. These experiences have sparked interest among paranormal enthusiasts, prompting investigations and explorations into the site's ghostly history.

As visitors embark on ghost tours throughout Albuquerque, they are not merely spectators to these tales but participants in the living history of the city. Each story shared by residents adds depth and authenticity to the experience, bridging the gap between the past and present. Whether it's a whispered warning from the spirit of a lost soul or the playful antics of a mischievous ghost, these narratives enrich the cultural landscape of Albuquerque, making it a captivating destination for those intrigued by the paranormal.

Famous Hauntings and Their Histories

Albuquerque is steeped in rich history, with a tapestry of stories woven through its streets, many of which include tales of hauntings and the supernatural. One of the most famous locations is the Albuquerque Old Town Plaza. Established in 1706, this area has seen countless events, from celebrations to tragedies. Visitors often report feeling cold spots and hearing whispers that seem to echo from the past. The historic structures, including the San Felipe de Neri Church, are said to house spirits of those who once walked these grounds, creating a palpable energy that draws ghost enthusiasts and curious travelers alike.

The Hotel Andaluz, a stunning establishment that dates back to the 1920s, is another hotspot for paranormal activity. Originally built as a luxury hotel, it has maintained its charm and elegance while also becoming a focal point for ghost stories. Guests have recounted experiences of seeing apparitions in period dress wandering the halls. Staff members have shared encounters with a playful spirit known to rearrange furniture and leave the sound of laughter lingering in the air. The hotel's storied past and luxurious ambiance make it a compelling destination for those seeking a touch of the supernatural.

Another notable haunting is associated with the Albuquerque High School, known for its rich history and architectural beauty. The school, which opened in 1892, has witnessed several tragedies over the years, including accidents and untimely deaths. These events have led to reports of ghostly figures appearing in the hallways, particularly in the old gymnasium. Students and faculty alike have shared tales of unexplained noises, flickering lights, and the sensation of being watched. The presence of these spirits has made the high school a point of intrigue for local ghost tours, adding to the lore of Albuquerque's haunted locations.

The La Posada de Albuquerque is another establishment that boasts a haunted reputation. Once a stop for travelers along the Santa Fe Trail, this historic hotel has its share of ghostly encounters. Guests have reported strange occurrences such as doors opening on their own and the faint sounds of music playing in empty rooms. Many believe that the spirits of former guests linger to relive their journeys, and the hotel's rich history as a gathering place has contributed to its reputation as a paranormal hotspot.

Finally, the Sandia Mountains, with their rugged beauty, also harbor their own ghostly legends. These mountains are said to be home to the spirits of Native American tribes who once roamed the area. Hikers and outdoor enthusiasts have reported seeing shadowy figures and hearing whispers carried by the wind. The mountains' history, combined with the reverence of the land, creates an atmosphere ripe for supernatural encounters. Many ghost tours incorporate these natural wonders, inviting adventurers to explore not only the haunted sites of Albuquerque but the mystical energies that the surrounding landscape offers.

Chapter 6: Seasonal Ghost Tours and Events

Halloween Specials

Halloween in Albuquerque offers a unique blend of tradition, culture, and the supernatural, making it an ideal time for ghost tours and paranormal adventures. As the air turns crisp and the nights grow longer, the city transforms into a playground for those seeking thrills and chills. Numerous tour companies curate special Halloween events that delve into the city's haunted history, inviting participants to explore the eerie tales that have shaped Albuquerque's reputation as a hub of paranormal activity.

One of the highlights of Halloween specials in Albuquerque is the themed ghost tours that occur throughout October. These tours often feature enhanced narratives, focusing on local legends and infamous hauntings. Participants can expect to visit sites such as the historic Old Town Plaza, where ghostly apparitions and unexplained phenomena have been reported for generations. Storytellers guide guests through the cobblestone streets, regaling them with spine-tingling stories of past residents and the restless spirits said to linger in the shadows.

In addition to traditional ghost tours, Halloween also brings unique experiences like haunted house attractions and paranormal investigations. Many tour companies host special events where participants can use ghost-hunting equipment, such as EMF meters and spirit boxes, to try and make contact with the other side. These immersive experiences allow visitors to engage directly with the paranormal, offering a thrilling opportunity to learn about the science and folklore surrounding ghost hunting while exploring some of Albuquerque's most haunted locations.

Food and drink play a pivotal role in Albuquerque's Halloween celebrations, with many establishments offering spooky-themed menus and craft cocktails. Ghost tours often include stops at local bars and restaurants, where guests can enjoy seasonal treats while listening to stories of hauntings associated with each venue. This combination of culinary delights and ghostly tales enhances the overall experience, creating a festive atmosphere that celebrates both the holiday and the rich history of the area.

As Halloween approaches, Albuquerque becomes a vibrant hub for those seeking the supernatural. The combination of haunted history, engaging storytelling, and immersive experiences creates a unique atmosphere that attracts both locals and tourists. Whether you are a seasoned ghost hunter or simply curious about the paranormal, the Halloween specials in Albuquerque offer a thrilling adventure that captures the spirit of the season and the essence of the city's haunted past.

Ghost Tours During the Holidays

Ghost tours during the holidays in Albuquerque offer a unique blend of festive cheer and spine-tingling thrills. As the city transforms into a winter wonderland, the narrative of its haunted history becomes even more captivating. Visitors can explore the rich folklore of the Southwest while marveling at the holiday decorations that adorn the historic buildings and streets. These tours typically take place in the evening, allowing participants to experience the enchanting atmosphere of the city draped in lights, all while delving into the supernatural tales that have shaped its past.

Many ghost tours in Albuquerque are designed to cater to the holiday spirit. Guides often incorporate seasonal themes, sharing ghostly legends tied to Christmas, New Year's, and other winter celebrations. For instance, tales of lost souls seeking redemption or spirits who once celebrated the holidays can provide a haunting yet poignant backdrop. This storytelling approach not only entertains but also invites participants to reflect on the significance of these traditions, adding depth to the experience. Engaging with the local lore during this festive time enhances the connection between history and the present.

One popular destination for ghost tours is Old Town Albuquerque, where the streets are lined with adobe buildings dating back to the 18th century. As guests stroll through its cobblestone paths, they are introduced to stories of spirits that linger among the festive decorations. The juxtaposition of holiday cheer and chilling tales creates a memorable experience. Visitors often report feeling an eerie presence as they stand in front of the San Felipe de Neri Church, where legends of spectral sightings abound. This blend of history, architecture, and ghostly encounters captures the essence of the Southwest's haunted heritage.

In addition to the standard ghost tours, many operators offer special holiday-themed experiences. Some tours may include hot cocoa or mulled wine, allowing guests to enjoy a warm beverage as they embark on their ghostly journey. Others might incorporate live music or performances, enhancing the overall ambiance. These additional elements help to create a festive atmosphere while maintaining the thrill of paranormal exploration. Participants are not just passive observers; they become part of the narrative, engaging with the stories as they walk in the footsteps of those who came before.

For those seeking a different kind of holiday adventure, ghost tours in Albuquerque provide an opportunity to embrace both the spooky and the cheerful. As travelers navigate the city's haunted past, they also create lasting memories with family and friends. The combination of holiday spirit and ghostly tales offers a unique way to experience Albuquerque, ensuring that the memories made during these tours will linger long after the holiday season has passed. Whether one is a seasoned ghost hunter or a curious traveler, these tours promise an unforgettable journey into the heart of the Southwest's supernatural legacy.

Year-Round Paranormal Events

Albuquerque, with its rich cultural tapestry and historical depth, serves as a prime location for year-round paranormal events that attract both locals and tourists alike. The unique blend of Native American heritage, Spanish colonial history, and modern influences creates an environment ripe for ghostly tales and supernatural experiences. Visitors to the city can participate in various events that explore the haunted history and enigmatic legends that have emerged from its past, making for a thrilling addition to any travel itinerary.

One of the most notable year-round events is the Albuquerque Ghost Tour, which invites participants to explore the city's haunted hotspots. Guided by knowledgeable storytellers, these tours delve into the spine-chilling stories of restless spirits that haunt local landmarks. Locations like the Old Town Plaza, reputedly home to several ghostly apparitions, come to life as guides recount tales of the past. These tours not only provide a glimpse into the supernatural but also highlight the rich history of Albuquerque, making them an ideal activity for history buffs and thrill-seekers alike.

Another exciting option for those interested in paranormal experiences is the Ghost Hunting 101 workshops held throughout the year. These events offer participants a hands-on opportunity to learn about ghost hunting techniques and tools used to communicate with spirits. Led by experienced paranormal investigators, attendees gain insights into the science of the supernatural, including how to use EMF detectors and spirit boxes. This interactive experience appeals to both skeptics and believers, providing a unique perspective on the world of the paranormal while fostering a sense of community among participants.

Additionally, Albuquerque hosts various themed events aligned with seasonal celebrations, enhancing the paranormal experience. During Halloween, for instance, special ghost tours and haunted happenings are organized that ramp up the excitement. These events often feature storytelling sessions, costume contests, and even live reenactments of famous ghostly encounters, creating an immersive atmosphere that captivates participants. Similarly, around Día de los Muertos, visitors can engage in events that honor the spirits of loved ones, providing a cultural perspective on death and the afterlife that resonates deeply with many.

Year-round paranormal events in Albuquerque not only entertain but also educate participants about the city's complex history and the stories that have shaped its identity. Engaging with the supernatural through tours, workshops, and seasonal celebrations allows visitors to explore the mysteries of the past while enjoying the vibrant culture of Albuquerque. Whether one is seeking a thrilling adventure or a deeper understanding of the spiritual realm, Albuquerque offers a diverse array of paranormal experiences that cater to all interests and preferences.

Chapter 7: Planning Your Ghost Tour Adventure

Tips for First-Time Ghost Tour Participants

When embarking on your first ghost tour in Albuquerque, preparation can significantly enhance your experience. Start by researching the specific tour you plan to join. Each ghost tour may focus on different aspects of the paranormal, from historic hauntings to local legends. Understanding the tour's theme can help set your expectations and increase your engagement. Familiarize yourself with the areas you will visit, including their history and any notable figures associated with them. Having a basic knowledge of Albuquerque's past will enrich your experience and help you connect more deeply with the stories shared by your guide.

Dress appropriately for the occasion, as ghost tours often take place in the evening and may involve walking or standing for extended periods. Comfortable shoes are essential, especially if the tour includes uneven terrain or cobblestone streets, which are common in historic districts. Be mindful of the weather; layers are a good idea in case temperatures drop after sunset. Bringing a light jacket or sweater can keep you comfortable as you delve into the chilling tales of the supernatural. Additionally, consider carrying a small flashlight to illuminate your path, particularly if the tour takes you to darker, less well-lit areas.

Engagement is key during a ghost tour. Many guides encourage participants to ask questions and share their own spooky experiences. Take advantage of this opportunity to interact with your guide and fellow participants. This not only makes the experience more enjoyable but can also lead to interesting discussions and insights that may not be part of the standard narrative. If you have any specific interests in the paranormal, share them with your guide; they may be able to tailor the experience or share additional stories that align with your interests.

Documenting your experience can be both fun and rewarding. Many tour participants enjoy taking photos or jotting down notes about the stories they hear. However, be respectful of the atmosphere and other participants by minimizing distractions. If you're hoping to capture any paranormal phenomena, familiarize yourself with your camera or smartphone's settings beforehand, especially if you're in low-light conditions. Remember that some locations may have restrictions on photography, so it's best to check with your guide before snapping away.

Finally, keep an open mind and embrace the unknown. Ghost tours are designed to entertain and educate, but individual experiences can vary greatly. Whether you're a skeptic or a believer, allow yourself to feel the ambiance of the locations you visit. The power of suggestion can evoke strong emotions, and many participants find themselves drawn into the stories being told. Enjoy the thrill of the experience and remember that the essence of a ghost tour lies not just in the stories but also in the atmosphere and the shared adventure with fellow ghost enthusiasts.

Best Times of Year to Visit

When planning a visit to Albuquerque for ghost tours and paranormal experiences, timing can greatly enhance the adventure. The best times of year to explore the haunted sites of this vibrant city often coincide with seasonal events and atmospheric conditions that heighten the thrill of ghost hunting. While Albuquerque offers rich paranormal opportunities year-round, certain periods stand out for their unique energy and enhanced experiences.

Autumn, particularly from late September to early November, is an ideal time to visit Albuquerque. The crisp air and vibrant foliage create an enchanting backdrop for ghost tours. October, with its Halloween festivities, attracts both locals and tourists seeking spine-tingling experiences. Haunted houses, ghost walks, and themed events abound during this time, making it a hub for those interested in the supernatural. The energy of the season seems to amplify the stories shared by guides, drawing visitors into the rich tapestry of local lore and legends.

Winter months, particularly December, can also provide a unique experience for ghost hunters. The holiday season casts a magical spell over the city, and the quieter streets create a more intimate atmosphere for exploring haunted sites. Many ghost tours operate during this time, offering a different perspective on the paranormal. The contrast of chilly nights against the warmth of historic venues enhances the thrill of the unknown, and the stories of spirits lingering in festive settings can be particularly captivating.

Spring, especially in March and April, brings a resurgence of life and energy to Albuquerque. As the weather warms, so does the spirit of exploration. This season often sees an uptick in ghost tour offerings, with guides eager to share fresh stories and experiences with visitors. The blooming landscape and clearer skies can make evening tours particularly enjoyable, allowing for a vivid connection to the haunted histories of the city. Springtime also aligns with various cultural events, providing opportunities to delve deeper into the local traditions that intertwine with the supernatural.

Summer, while hot, presents its own set of advantages for ghostly adventures. The longer daylight hours allow for flexible scheduling, making it easier to fit in multiple tours or experiences. Evening tours often begin after sunset, when the heat of the day dissipates, and the thrill of the unknown can be felt more intensely. Local festivals and gatherings during this season also offer a chance to meet fellow paranormal enthusiasts, enhancing the overall experience. While summer may not be the primary season for ghostly tales, the vibrant atmosphere of Albuquerque creates a unique setting for those willing to brave the heat in search of spirits.

Preparing for a Paranormal Experience

When preparing for a paranormal experience in Albuquerque, the first step is to conduct thorough research on the locations you plan to visit. Albuquerque is rich in history, with many sites known for their ghostly encounters and supernatural lore. Familiarizing yourself with the stories associated with each site can enhance your experience, as you will have a deeper understanding of the spirits that may linger there. Look for reputable ghost tour companies that offer insightful narratives and ensure that they are knowledgeable about both the history and the paranormal activities of the area.

Physical preparation is also essential when embarking on a ghost tour. Wear comfortable clothing and sturdy shoes, as many tours involve walking through historical districts or uneven terrain. The climate in Albuquerque can be unpredictable, so it is wise to check the weather forecast and dress accordingly. Bring along essentials such as water, a flashlight, and a notebook for jotting down any experiences or observations. If you have a camera or audio recording device, consider bringing them as well, as they can help capture any unexplained phenomena you may encounter.

Mental preparation is equally important when engaging in paranormal activities. Approach the experience with an open mind and a respectful attitude toward the spirits you may encounter. Some individuals may feel apprehensive or skeptical, and it's crucial to find a mindset that fosters curiosity rather than fear. Practices such as meditation or mindfulness can help center your thoughts, allowing you to be more present during the tour. Engaging in discussions with fellow participants can also create a supportive environment for sharing personal beliefs and experiences related to the paranormal.

Additionally, consider the time of year for your visit. Certain periods, such as Halloween or the Day of the Dead, may offer unique events or heightened paranormal activity. Participating in local festivities can enrich your experience and provide context to the ghost stories and legends that permeate the area.

During these times, many tours may include special presentations or guest speakers who can share their insights into the supernatural aspects of Albuquerque's culture.

Finally, remember to document your experience after the tour. Reflecting on your thoughts and feelings about the events can provide closure and help solidify your memories. Sharing your experiences with friends or online communities interested in the paranormal can also foster connections with others who share your enthusiasm. Whether you encounter a ghostly presence or simply enjoy the thrill of the unknown, preparing thoughtfully for your paranormal adventure in Albuquerque will enhance your overall experience and create lasting memories.

Chapter 8: Beyond Ghost Tours: Other Paranormal Activities

Exploring Haunted Hotels

Haunted hotels are not just places to stay; they are gateways to the past, where the echoes of history linger in the hallways and whisper through the walls. Albuquerque, rich in culture and history, boasts several hotels that have earned their reputation as haunted destinations. For those intrigued by the paranormal, these sites offer more than just accommodations; they provide an opportunity to experience the unexplained, meet the spirits of the past, and perhaps even witness a ghostly encounter. Exploring haunted hotels in Albuquerque can add an exciting layer to your travel experience, blending comfort with a touch of the supernatural.

One of the most notable haunted hotels in Albuquerque is the Hotel Andaluz. This historic hotel, originally built in the 1920s, has preserved its Spanish Colonial architecture and charm while embracing modern amenities. Guests have reported strange occurrences, such as flickering lights, unexplained cold spots, and the sensation of being watched. The spirit of a former guest, who is believed to have passed away in the hotel, is said to roam the halls, adding an eerie atmosphere to the otherwise elegant environment. Those who stay here can enjoy both the rich history of the building and the thrill of potential ghostly encounters.

Another intriguing venue is the El Rey Court, a boutique hotel that has attracted both travelers and spirits alike. With its unique blend of Southwestern style and vintage flair, guests have often shared stories of strange noises, disembodied laughter, and even sightings of ghostly figures in the courtyard. The history of the El Rey Court is deeply intertwined with Albuquerque's past, and the hotel has become a hotspot for paranormal investigations. Whether you are lounging by the pool or enjoying a meal at the on-site restaurant, the possibility of encountering a spirit adds an exciting edge to your stay.

For those seeking a more immersive experience, the Albuquerque Inn & Spa at Old Town provides a charming setting steeped in history and mystery. This inn is located near Old Town, a historic area filled with shops and galleries, and has been the site of numerous ghostly sightings. Visitors have reported seeing apparitions in their rooms and hearing footsteps in the hallways late at night. The inn's dedication to preserving its historic roots makes it an ideal place for those interested in the paranormal, as it offers both a cozy retreat and a chance to connect with the spirits that may still inhabit the space.

When exploring haunted hotels in Albuquerque, it is essential to approach the experience with an open mind and a sense of adventure. Each location has its unique stories and legends, enticing travelers to delve deeper into the mysteries of the past. Ghost tours often include visits to these haunted hotels, allowing guests to learn about the spirits that linger and the history that surrounds them. Whether you are a seasoned ghost hunter or simply curious about the supernatural, these hotels provide an unforgettable blend of history, intrigue, and the chance to connect with the unseen world.

Paranormal Retreats and Workshops

Paranormal retreats and workshops have gained popularity in Albuquerque, attracting those eager to explore the mystical and supernatural realms. These experiences offer participants a unique opportunity to delve into the world of ghosts, spirits, and other phenomena, often in historically rich locations that enhance the overall atmosphere. Whether you are a seasoned ghost hunter or a curious beginner, these retreats provide a comprehensive look at the methods, tools, and techniques used in paranormal investigations. Workshops typically include a mix of lectures, hands-on activities, and guided investigations, making them perfect for individuals seeking both education and adventure.

Many paranormal retreats in Albuquerque are hosted in venues known for their haunted histories, such as old hotels, historic homes, and even abandoned buildings. These locations not only set the mood but also provide participants with real-life opportunities to experience the paranormal. As you engage in activities such as EVP (Electronic Voice Phenomena) sessions, spirit box communications, and ghost hunting with specialized equipment, you will learn how to interpret the findings and understand the stories behind the spirits that may linger in these spaces. The combination of education and practical experience makes these retreats a compelling choice for those intrigued by the unknown.

In addition to ghost hunting techniques, these workshops often explore the cultural and historical contexts of the spirits encountered. Participants gain insights into local folklore, legends, and the significance of various sites within Albuquerque. This educational aspect enriches the experience, allowing individuals to appreciate the deeper connections between the living and the spirits of the past. Many instructors are well-versed in both history and the paranormal, providing a balanced perspective that enhances the learning process. This approach ensures that attendees leave not only with new skills but also with a greater appreciation for the cultural heritage of the Southwest.

Social interaction is another valuable component of paranormal retreats. Participants often come from diverse backgrounds, creating an environment ripe for sharing experiences and forging connections. The camaraderie fostered during shared investigations can lead to lasting friendships, and many individuals find themselves returning to reconnect with fellow enthusiasts. This sense of community is particularly important in a field often viewed as niche, as it allows participants to feel supported in their interests and pursuits. Networking with like-minded individuals can also open doors to future collaborations or adventures in the paranormal realm.

For those seeking a deeper engagement with the supernatural, paranormal retreats and workshops in Albuquerque offer an enriching experience that combines learning, exploration, and community. With the backdrop of the city's haunted history, these events allow participants to immerse themselves fully in the world of spirits and the unknown. Whether attending for personal enrichment, entertainment, or a combination of both, these retreats provide an unforgettable way to explore the enigmatic and often thrilling aspects of the paranormal.

Utilizing Social Media and Online Resources

Utilizing social media and online resources can enhance your experience when exploring the ghost tours and paranormal adventures in Albuquerque. With a vibrant online community dedicated to the supernatural, platforms like Facebook, Instagram, and Twitter serve as valuable tools for gaining insights into local ghostly happenings, upcoming events, and personal experiences shared by fellow enthusiasts. Engaging with these platforms allows travelers to connect with like-minded individuals, gather recommendations, and stay informed about any new or seasonal tours that may not be widely advertised.

One effective way to utilize social media is by following local ghost tour companies and paranormal organizations. Many of these entities actively post updates, special offers, and behind-the-scenes content that can deepen your understanding of the local haunted history. Additionally, social media groups focused on paranormal investigations and ghost hunting provide a space for discussions, where members share their experiences and tips. This interaction can lead to discovering lesser-known locations and hidden gems that might not appear in conventional tourist guides.

Online resources such as blogs, podcasts, and YouTube channels dedicated to paranormal investigations can also enrich your knowledge about Albuquerque's haunted past. Many content creators share detailed accounts of their ghost hunts, providing insights into the techniques they use and the stories behind various locations. This supplementary information can prepare you for your own ghost tour, allowing you to ask informed questions and engage more deeply with the guides and their narratives.

Review sites like TripAdvisor or Yelp are invaluable for reading firsthand accounts from previous participants. These platforms allow potential visitors to assess the quality of tours and experiences based on the reviews and ratings left by others. Pay attention to comments regarding the guides' expertise, the authenticity of the experiences, and any unique features that might make one tour stand out from the rest. Such insights can help you select the most appealing options for your paranormal adventure.

Finally, consider leveraging online event platforms such as Eventbrite or Meetup to find unique paranormal events and gatherings happening during your visit. These platforms often list special events, workshops, or even ghost-themed parties that can provide a more immersive experience. Participating in these gatherings not only adds to your adventure but also expands your network within the paranormal community, allowing you to meet others who share your interests while exploring the haunted allure of Albuquerque.

Chapter 9: The Cultural Impact of Ghost Stories

Ghost Stories in Local Culture

Ghost stories have long been an integral part of local culture in Albuquerque, intertwining history, folklore, and the supernatural. The city, with its rich tapestry of Native American, Spanish, and Mexican heritage, serves as a backdrop for numerous ghostly tales that have been passed down through generations. These stories reflect the beliefs, fears, and experiences of the people who have called this region home. As visitors embark on ghost tours, they not only explore the spooky side of Albuquerque but also gain insights into the cultural significance of these narratives.

One of the most notable ghost stories in Albuquerque centers around the historic Old Town Plaza. This area, with its cobblestone streets and centuries-old adobe buildings, is said to be haunted by the spirits of settlers and Native Americans alike. Visitors often report strange occurrences, such as unexplained cold spots and the feeling of being watched. The stories of La Llorona, a weeping woman said to roam the Rio Grande in search of her lost children, resonate deeply within the local community. These tales connect the past with the present, illustrating how folklore continues to shape the cultural identity of Albuquerque.

The Sandia Mountains, which loom over the city, also play a significant role in local ghost stories. Many residents believe that the spirits of ancient Puebloans still roam the mountains, guarding sacred sites and watching over the land. Ghostly apparitions and eerie sounds have been reported by hikers and outdoor enthusiasts, adding to the mystique of the area. This connection to nature and spirituality is a theme that runs through many local ghost stories, emphasizing the reverence that Albuquerque's residents have for their environment and its history.

Ghost tours in Albuquerque often feature sites like the former New Mexico State Penitentiary, known for its violent past and reported hauntings. The infamous 1980 riot, which resulted in the deaths of many inmates, has led to numerous accounts of ghostly encounters within the prison walls. Tour guides recount chilling experiences shared by former staff and visitors, including disembodied voices and shadowy figures. These narratives not only provide thrills for those seeking a paranormal experience but also serve as a reminder of the complex history and societal issues that have shaped Albuquerque.

As tourists explore the ghostly tales of the city, they engage with the rich cultural heritage that underpins these stories. The blend of historical events, local legends, and the supernatural creates a unique experience for visitors. By participating in ghost tours, travelers not only seek thrills but also gain a deeper understanding of Albuquerque's past. The spirit of the city remains alive through these stories, ensuring that the ghosts of Albuquerque continue to intrigue and haunt those who wander its streets.

The Role of Ghost Tours in Tourism

Ghost tours have become an essential component of the tourism landscape, particularly in cities rich with history and folklore like Albuquerque. These tours offer visitors a unique opportunity to explore the darker aspects of local culture and history while engaging with the supernatural. They often blend storytelling with historical facts, providing a captivating experience that appeals not only to paranormal enthusiasts but also to those looking to learn more about the city and its past. The allure of ghostly encounters draws in a diverse crowd, making these tours a popular choice for adults seeking something beyond the traditional sightseeing experience.

In Albuquerque, ghost tours typically take participants through some of the city's most haunted locations, each with its own tales of tragedy, mystery, and spectral sightings. These sites often include historic buildings, old cemeteries, and landmarks known for their eerie atmospheres. As guides recount chilling stories and local legends, tourists gain insight into the historical events that shaped the city and its inhabitants. This combination of education and entertainment not only enhances the visitor's understanding of Albuquerque's history but also fosters a deeper connection to the place they are exploring.

The rise of ghost tourism has also had significant economic implications for Albuquerque. Local businesses, such as restaurants, shops, and hotels, benefit from the influx of visitors who participate in ghost tours. These tours often lead to increased foot traffic in the areas they cover, encouraging tourists to explore additional attractions in the vicinity. This symbiotic relationship between ghost tours and local commerce highlights the potential for niche tourism markets to contribute positively to the economy, creating jobs and supporting community initiatives.

Additionally, ghost tours promote cultural exchange and storytelling, key elements in preserving local heritage. Many tours are led by knowledgeable guides who share their passion for Albuquerque's history and folklore. This personal touch not only enriches the tour experience but also fosters an appreciation for the narratives that define the city. By engaging with these stories, tourists are invited to participate in a living history, allowing them to take home a piece of Albuquerque's cultural identity that goes beyond mere souvenirs.

Finally, ghost tours serve as a platform for discussions surrounding the paranormal and the afterlife, providing a space for individuals to explore their beliefs and experiences. They encourage open-mindedness and curiosity, prompting participants to question the boundaries between the known and the unknown. As visitors share their own stories and encounters, a communal atmosphere develops, reinforcing the idea that everyone has a story to tell. This connection not only enhances the tour experience but also cultivates a community of like-minded individuals drawn together by their fascination with the mystical aspects of life. Through ghost tours, Albuquerque not only showcases its haunted past but also invites travelers to engage with it in a meaningful way.

Ghost Stories as a Means of Preservation

Ghost stories have long served as a powerful tool for cultural preservation, particularly in regions rich in history and folklore like Albuquerque. These narratives, often steeped in local legend, not only entertain but also encapsulate the values, fears, and beliefs of the communities that share them. In Albuquerque, ghost stories invite individuals into a deeper understanding of the city's past, revealing the layers of experiences that have shaped its identity. From tales of haunted buildings to the spirits of historical figures, these stories preserve the essence of the city's cultural heritage and provide a unique lens through which to view its history.

The act of storytelling itself is a communal ritual, often passed down through generations, which reinforces social bonds among community members. In Albuquerque, ghost tours offer an interactive experience where participants can engage with both the stories and the locations associated with them. As guides share chilling accounts of hauntings and unexplained phenomena, they also weave in historical context that connects the audience to the city's past. This connection not only keeps the stories alive but also instills a sense of pride and belonging among those who call Albuquerque home, as well as those visiting.

In the context of preservation, ghost stories also serve to highlight lesser-known aspects of history that may be overlooked in traditional narratives. For instance, the tales of marginalized individuals or events that were not officially documented come to life through these eerie accounts. They offer a platform for voices that have been silenced and allow new generations to explore the complexities of their heritage. By bringing these stories into the limelight, ghost tours and paranormal experiences encourage a broader understanding of Albuquerque's multifaceted history and the societal dynamics that have shaped it.

Moreover, ghost stories contribute to the tourism industry, drawing visitors who are eager to engage with the supernatural. This influx of tourists not only boosts the local economy but also creates opportunities for local storytellers and historians to share their knowledge. As visitors participate in ghost tours, they become part of a living tradition that honors and preserves the cultural narratives of Albuquerque. Their experiences can encourage further exploration of the city's history, prompting a deeper appreciation for the past and its ongoing influence on the present.

Ultimately, ghost stories in Albuquerque are more than mere entertainment; they are vital narratives that help preserve the city's cultural legacy. By participating in ghost tours and exploring paranormal experiences, individuals contribute to the ongoing dialogue about history, memory, and identity. These stories serve as a bridge between the past and the present, ensuring that the spirits of Albuquerque—both literal and metaphorical—continue to resonate with future generations. In this way, ghost stories become a means of preservation, keeping alive the rich tapestry of experiences that define the Southwest.

Chapter 10: Conclusion: Embracing the Paranormal

The Significance of Ghost Tours

Ghost tours have become a significant aspect of the cultural landscape in many cities, and Albuquerque is no exception. These tours offer a unique blend of history, folklore, and the supernatural, appealing to both locals and visitors seeking an engaging way to explore the city. They provide an opportunity to delve into the rich tapestry of Albuquerque's past, uncovering stories that may be overlooked in traditional historical narratives. By highlighting the darker, often forgotten moments of history, ghost tours encourage participants to reflect on the complexities of the human experience.

The significance of ghost tours extends beyond mere entertainment; they serve as a conduit for cultural education. Many of the tales shared during these experiences are rooted in the lives of real people, events, and places, allowing participants to connect with Albuquerque's heritage on a deeper level. The stories of spirits wandering the streets or haunting historic buildings often come with lessons about the struggles, triumphs, and tragedies that shaped the community. This storytelling aspect fosters a sense of connection to the past, providing a more nuanced understanding of the city and its inhabitants.

Moreover, ghost tours often highlight the unique architectural and historical landmarks of Albuquerque, inviting guests to appreciate the city's beauty from a different perspective. As participants walk through the streets at night, they encounter the atmospheric charm of historic buildings, which take on an even more captivating presence when viewed through the lens of ghostly tales. This immersive experience enhances the appreciation of Albuquerque's cultural and architectural heritage, encouraging visitors to return and explore further during the daytime.

The appeal of ghost tours is also rooted in their ability to create a shared experience among participants. As adults embark on these nocturnal adventures, they bond over their shared curiosity about the paranormal and the mysteries of the unknown. Whether traveling with friends or meeting new people, the thrill of exploring haunted sites fosters camaraderie and sparks intriguing conversations. This social aspect adds an additional layer of enjoyment, making ghost tours an ideal activity for vacationers seeking memorable experiences.

Finally, the significance of ghost tours lies in their ability to engage with the broader themes of fear, curiosity, and the unknown. They provide a safe space for individuals to confront their fears and explore the supernatural in a controlled environment. For many, the allure of the paranormal is not just about seeking out ghosts but about understanding the boundaries between life and death, reality and imagination. By participating in ghost tours, individuals not only entertain the possibility of encountering spirits but also engage in a deeper exploration of their own beliefs and perceptions, making these experiences profoundly impactful.

Reflections on the Paranormal Experience

The allure of the paranormal has captivated humans for centuries, and in Albuquerque, this fascination takes on a unique flavor. The city's rich history, steeped in Native American culture and Spanish colonial heritage, provides a perfect backdrop for ghost tours and paranormal adventures. Visitors often find themselves drawn to the stories of lost spirits and haunted locations that echo the past. These experiences not only entertain but also provoke thought about the nature of existence, life after death, and our connection to the supernatural.

As guests embark on ghost tours, they are often greeted by local guides who are both knowledgeable and passionate about the area's haunted history. These storytellers weave narratives filled with personal anecdotes, historical facts, and chilling encounters that pique the interest of even the most skeptical participants. Walking through shadowy streets and ancient buildings, tourists are invited to step outside their comfort zones and explore the possibility of the unknown. This interaction with the paranormal can lead to profound reflections on one's beliefs and perceptions of reality.

The emotional impact of a paranormal experience can be profound. Many participants report feelings of unease, excitement, or even catharsis as they confront the stories of those who have come before. For some, the idea of ghosts serves as a reminder of loved ones who have passed away, creating a sense of connection that transcends time. The shared experience of witnessing something inexplicable fosters camaraderie among participants, transforming a simple tour into a collective journey through the unknown.

Albuquerque's haunted sites, from the historic Old Town to the eerie remnants of the Sandia Mountains, offer a diverse range of experiences that cater to various interests. Many locations are steeped in cultural significance, allowing visitors to gain insight into the beliefs and practices of those who once inhabited the land. Engaging with these sites encourages a deeper understanding of the interplay between history and the supernatural, prompting reflections on how past traumas and experiences continue to resonate in the present.

Ultimately, the exploration of the paranormal in Albuquerque serves as a reminder of the mysteries that life holds. While not everyone may encounter a ghost or feel the presence of a spirit, the journey through these haunted locales invites contemplation and curiosity. The stories shared during ghost tours allow participants to confront their fears and expand their understanding of what lies beyond the physical realm. In doing so, they may discover that the true essence of the paranormal experience is not merely about ghosts, but about the connections we forge with our histories and each other.

Encouragement to Explore and Discover

Exploring the haunted landscapes of Albuquerque presents a unique opportunity for adventure seekers and paranormal enthusiasts alike. The city is steeped in rich history, where the past intertwines with the present, creating a tapestry of ghostly tales and unexplained phenomena. From the storied streets of Old Town to the eerie remnants of abandoned buildings, each corner of Albuquerque offers something intriguing for those willing to venture into the unknown.

One of the most compelling aspects of Albuquerque's ghost tours is the chance to uncover the true stories behind the city's spirited inhabitants. Guided by knowledgeable hosts, participants are taken on a journey through time, where they can learn about the events that shaped the region and the spirits that still linger. These narratives often reveal the personal struggles and triumphs of those who lived in Albuquerque long ago, providing a deeper understanding of the city's cultural heritage while connecting visitors with the supernatural.

The thrill of the unknown is a significant draw for many who seek out paranormal experiences. Whether you're a skeptic or a believer, the excitement of walking through haunted sites can awaken a sense of wonder and curiosity. Visitors are encouraged to keep an open mind as they navigate through the stories and legends of Albuquerque, as they may find themselves experiencing something inexplicable. Each tour offers a blend of history, folklore, and personal anecdotes, which can lead to unexpected moments of connection with the supernatural.

As adventurers delve into the paranormal landscape, they will discover that these experiences can foster a sense of community. Joining a ghost tour or participating in paranormal investigations allows individuals to bond over shared interests, creating lasting memories and friendships. The camaraderie built during these explorations can enhance the experience, as participants share their thoughts, fears, and encounters, enriching the overall adventure.

Ultimately, the encouragement to explore and discover in Albuquerque's haunted realms is an invitation to embrace the mysteries that surround us. Whether you are drawn to the thrill of ghost hunting or the allure of historical narratives, the city's paranormal offerings provide a gateway to understanding the complexities of life, death, and the spirits that inhabit the spaces in between. Embrace the adventure and allow yourself to be captivated by the stories and experiences that await in the heart of the Southwest.

Don't miss out!

Visit the website below and you can sign up to receive emails whenever Stephen G. publishes a new book. There's no charge and no obligation.

https://books2read.com/r/B-A-VPPMC-XWGBF